What We Did Before Our Moth Days

Wallace Shawn's first play to be produced in New York was *Our Late Night*, directed by André Gregory at the Public Theater in 1975. *A Thought in Three Parts* was staged two years later by the Joint Stock Theatre Group in London, directed by Max Stafford-Clark. His next three plays – *Marie and Bruce*, *Aunt Dan and Lemon* and *The Fever* – were all performed in New York at the Public Theater and in London at the Royal Court. *The Designated Mourner* premiered at the National Theatre, London, under the direction of David Hare, and was then performed in New York under the direction of André Gregory. In 2009, under Dominic Cooke's guidance, the Royal Court held a Wallace Shawn season, reviving *Aunt Dan and Lemon* and *The Fever*, and staging the premiere of *Grasses of a Thousand Colours*. Shawn also wrote the libretto for Allen Shawn's opera *The Music Teacher*, which was produced in New York by Scott Elliott's company The New Group. With André Gregory, he wrote the screenplay for the film *My Dinner with André*. With Tom Cairns, he wrote the screenplay for the film *Marie and Bruce*. And with Henrik Ibsen, he wrote the screenplay for the film *A Master Builder*. Shawn's book of essays, *Sleeping Among Sheep Under a Starry Sky*, is published by Europa Editions UK. It incorporates *Essays* and *Night Thoughts*, both published by Haymarket Books. His latest play, *What We Did Before Our Moth Days*, is scheduled to be produced in 2026 in New York.

by the same author from Faber

PLAYS ONE
(*A Thought in Three Parts, Marie and Bruce, Aunt Dan and Lemon, The Fever*)

THE DESIGNATED MOURNER
EVENING AT THE TALK HOUSE
THE FEVER

WALLACE SHAWN

What We Did Before Our Moth Days

faber

First published in 2025
by Faber and Faber Limited
The Bindery, 51 Hatton Garden
London, EC1N 8HN

Typeset by Brighton Gray
Printed in Canada

A CIP record for this book
is available from the British Library

ISBN 978-0-571-39990-1

FSC www.fsc.org MIX Paper | Supporting responsible forestry FSC® C103567

4 6 8 10 9 7 5 3

The world premiere of **What We Did Before Our Moth Days** was produced by Scott Rudin, Barry Diller, and Wallace Shawn at the Greenwich House Theater, New York City, and opened on March 5, 2026. The cast was as follows:

Elaine Hope Davis
Elle Maria Dizzia
Tim John Early
Dick Josh Hamilton

Director André Gregory
Scenic and Costume Designer Riccardo Hernandez
Lighting Designer Jennifer Tipton
Sound Designer Bruce Odland
Projection Designer Bill Morrison
Stage Managers Melanie T. Morgan & Lucas Kane
Production Manager Aurora Productions
General Manager DR Theatrical Management

Characters

Tim
twenty-five

Elaine
forty-five-ish

Elle
forty-five

Dick
forty-five

(*Suggested ages*)

WHAT WE DID BEFORE OUR MOTH DAYS

Production Note

At the beginning, the four characters appear together.

After they speak, Tim, Elaine, and Elle disappear for a while, leaving Dick alone.

Then, up until the end, the staging is whatever you want it to be.

I

Tim The thought did occur to me after we pulled into my garage that simply by sitting there for a while and failing to turn off the car's ignition I could perhaps inspire a curious story on the local radio station – something along the lines of, you know, 'Unfortunately, the police have still not uncovered the specific motivation that drove these two obviously desperate young people to end their lives in a sordid corner of Wood Street last night, but sadly, we fear that the . . .'

He chuckles for a while.

My car's exhaust system had long ago fallen into a state in which it could almost be considered a waste of a valuable resource not to use it for some sort of asphyxiation, and the venting pipe in my garage had clearly been recognized even longer ago as the most desirable place to go to in the neighborhood if you were a squirrel or a rat or a large bug and you felt that death was catching up to you and you were looking for a comfortable quiet corner in which to lie down and let it take you. The last time I looked, it was crowded in there! My companion sat beside me in the same state of composed passivity that she'd been in since we'd met in a gloomy part of the big city an hour earlier, and I found it hard to imagine that her demeanor would change or that she would raise any objection at all if the garage had suddenly begun to fill up even with the kind of gas that painfully burns the throat. At any rate, after a brief period of somewhat blissful silence, I exerted my will on myself, turned off the ignition, decisively opened the driver's side door, and stepped out of the car. Pushing a few boxes brusquely aside with my feet, treating them as if they'd never been alive and deserved no respect at all – which was true – I made my way to the passenger's side door, and let out my passenger. She was wearing a dark blue velvet dress. Then I unlocked the back entrance to my tiny house and led her into the small, cramped room that contained my refrigerator and various crates of food, as well as the card table with the lamp on it and a couple of chairs. My sense of smell had never been acute, so I honestly had never had any idea if the room smelled bad or not. I knew it didn't look very attractive. I myself would not have wanted to sit on either of the unpleasant chairs without my clothes on, and I certainly never did so, but my new companion immediately took off everything she was wearing, folded each item in a childlike manner, placed them all neatly on the card table next to the lamp, and sat down on the red chair. Naturally she had no way of knowing that I was judging the present moment to be one of the two or three high points in my life so far. Her nakedness, and its sudden appearance in my house, dizzied me. I felt light-headed – almost wobbly. Then Mickey, my very old, very large dog, wandered into the room and tentatively approached her and examined her, and she shocked me by patting him calmly on the head. She clearly was comfortable with dogs. As she and I had no language in common, I wasn't able to offer her any sort of pre-emptive apology or explanation concerning the possible physiological or psychological issues that might cause me to behave unexpectedly in regard to some of the classically celebrated acts in the canon of normal sexual behavior – I mean, of course I knew that she hadn't come to my house to pursue pleasure for herself in any event, but I didn't want her to feel she was obliged to do anything in particular to help me . . . and of course, for me at any rate, the main event had already just happened, although she didn't know that . . . And actually I would also have liked to try to express to her what her nakedness meant to me, in case that would have somehow pleased her, though who knows what she might have felt if I could have done so – but that wasn't possible either. Still, I did decide that even though it might be asinine, I would use my own language to offer her something to drink, so I put a glass in front of her and held up a couple of different bottles, while saying a bunch of meaningless words. She did get the point and quietly replied, in my language, 'No thank you.' And so then after that, I guided her through another door into the room that held my bed, and she sat down on it and waited for me to do something. I closed the door, leaving Mickey outside, flipped the switch that turned on an oddly placed bare bulb on the ceiling, stepped out of my moccasins, removed my trousers, and then with an almost unbelievably manly and virile gesture, I pulled down my underwear and threw it across the room, leaving my astounding member fully exposed. Then I took off my shirt and joined her on the bed, wondering vaguely if my member would terrify her. For a weird long moment I stared at her breasts, then even at her genitals, in a frank way I never could have done with a woman I knew, and I touched her very briefly, provoking no reaction, and then I took her hand and placed it very deliberately on my member, which now looked very dark in the shadows we cast, and she understood what I wanted, but it clearly wasn't something she was confident about, so at a certain point I very gently removed her hand, and then I lay on top of her and pressed myself against her until I came. And then I held her in my arms, hugging her close and feeling, 'Yes, I love her,' and I imagined myself driving her away from the violence and horror that I thought very probably went on inside the grim building from which I'd picked her up and to which I'd planned to return her – I imagined myself driving her away from that building and starting a whole new life with her. And then the phone rang, and it was Mother telling me that Father had died, and as I held the phone to my ear, I was still leaking semen onto my new companion's belly, and I remembered that Mahatma Gandhi in his autobiography had written about a somewhat similar experience he'd been involved in at the time of his own father's death. I wanted to lie there in the bed with my new companion, I wanted to hold her and hold on to her – and I was sort of furious that my father's death had to happen at this particular moment, and sad and bitter about it – but I felt I had no choice, I would have to bring my companion directly back to the unpleasant building where I'd found her, so that I could then go on to the center of the city to comfort my mother and deal with my father's death, all without being able to explain to my new friend in any way why I was suddenly in such a peculiar hurry.

When we arrived at the street where we'd first met earlier that evening, we both stepped out of the car, and I stood by her on the sidewalk as she rang a doorbell. There was a little melodious ding. And then an older woman opened the door, and as my companion stepped through the door and waved awkwardly at me, and I waved back, I was surprised to hear from inside the building the loud and painful crying of babies.

Then I got back in my car, but just before setting off for the familial apartment where my mother was now waiting alone with my father's body, I made a quick phone call to my best friend, a girl called Rapunzel whose house was just down the street from mine in the little town where I lived. I just had to tell her that my father had died. Rapunzel was a tall girl with a deep voice and a big face that looked partly like the face of a wolf and partly like the face of a calf, and as I was twenty-five and she was thirteen, there was an age difference there. Her parents were divorced, and she lived with her father, a disturbed and horrible man who would often pull me into his bedroom when I'd come to visit his daughter and keep me more or less imprisoned there as he passed on to me the latest facts about his love affair with a wealthy married woman whose frightening gluttony in regard to sex, he would explain to me rather frantically, his eyes darting wildly around the room, was so extreme as to be, he thought, possibly dangerous, medically, to him. It was as if he was looking to me for some sort of knowledge or wisdom about urology, which thank God I didn't have, but at any rate the good thing about his affair was that it meant that he was rarely at home, and so Rapunzel and I had the house to ourselves most of the time. Often, when I'd visit, she and I would play very simple card games, sometimes one game after another for hours at a time. But usually we'd just sit in her father's big armchairs, or on different sides of her father's enormous, empty desk, while she did homework and I worked on the designs for book covers by which I earned my humble living. Or else we'd sit in our armchairs and just quietly read, though quite frequently she'd be reading some enormously complicated nine-hundred-page nineteenth-century novel, while I'd be reading some not very profound or informative magazine article. We were a bit like two sheep grazing on the same hill – we were together, more or less, but we had no obligations to each other.

Elaine The elevator swayed crazily back and forth as it raced up, then it vomited me out into a tiny vestibule and went away fast. I rang a doorbell that made a repulsive buzzing sound, the door opened, and a young man with a pale face and a mustache was staring at me. Dick's son, Tim – it had to be. His eyes and mouth held no expression, and somehow because he was dressed all in white and was wearing some sort of sandals, my mind quickly flashed on blurry photographs of horror and violence in frightening corners of the world. I wasn't exactly attracted to him, but I had a momentary impulse to grab him by the shoulders. I suppressed my impulse, and then – yikes – there was Elle herself in the flesh. She was wearing a simple but elegant brown dress, standing absolutely motionless by the door of what had to be the bedroom, as if she were guarding it, and her face was bright red. An hour before, I'd heard her voice for the first time. I'd called Dick on the phone that she never answered, and, when she picked up, I knew what she would say, though her voice was different from the voice I'd always imagined she'd have. Now I felt sick, but all the same I went up to her, and I touched her arm, and I said, 'Please, I'm sorry, I need to see him.' She caught her breath and took a step back. I went into the room, and then she closed the door, or maybe she slammed it in a stifled sort of way. And there on an unmade bed in his wife's apartment my lover lay before me, face up in his pajamas, partly under the covers, but the expression on his face was one I'd never seen, a sort of half-grimace, that weird 'snapshot' look people have when a photograph catches them at the wrong moment, and yes, he was dead, all right. There was no ambiguity about it, as perhaps I'd expected there to be. He was simply a corpse. And there really wasn't anything I had to say to it, but almost because some ancient memory told me it was what one did, or it might be disrespectful or unloving not to do it, I kissed his forehead and then his utterly cold mouth, and then I opened the door and left the room. I touched Elle one more time, and then I touched young Tim, who was standing there next to her like a sort of accidentally frozen worm left behind in a person's refrigerator. His body felt almost as cold as his father's. He and I stared hard at each other, staring, staring, and then I let myself out of the apartment.

Elaine goes away.

Tim After the strange lady in the slinky yellow dress had left our apartment, Mother explained that she'd never met her either but that her name was Elaine. And then she explained to me who Elaine was. And then Mother and I went into the dark living room, she sat on a couch, I sat in a large armchair, and she talked to me about a lot of things. And I'd never thought that Mother was a very talkative person, but there was a lot of ground to cover. I lost track of time. But probably after we'd talked for an hour or so, some undertakers came and interrupted us. And was it upsetting to see them lifting poor Father up off the bed and zipping him into a garment bag and putting him on a gurney and taking him away? Yes, it was. It was extremely upsetting and unpleasant and sort of uncanny and unreal and not like anything else that had ever happened to me or to Mother, but nonetheless, as soon as they all went away and closed the front door, our conversation continued where it had left off, as if we'd been interrupted by something utterly trivial. The room was dark except for a couple of rather dim lamps, and Mother's face and dress looked purple.

Elle There was a story I read to Tim at bedtime more than once when he was a very young boy about the monkey god Hanuman, and I remembered how I'd felt when I read him the section in which Hanuman tore open his own chest with his bare hands to show the image that stood in his heart. And I remembered saying to Tim, 'You know, your father's image stands in my heart.'

Tim and Elle go away. Only Dick remains.

Dick When I was a boy, I never took death as seriously as I probably should have. My parents both had lots of older brothers and sisters, and somebody always seemed to be dying, and my mother was always miserable about it, and my father too would go into a melancholy mood on these occasions, and for whatever reason I was always irritated by their gloomy states of mind whenever somebody died, and I always found it vaguely absurd that they seemed to be so surprised every time that this event occurred, and so upset, when it seemed to me to be obviously one of the most common things to happen in the world – not to mention one of the most obviously boring things as well.

I'd probably figured out by the age of eight that everybody had many birthdays in the course of their life but only one day on which they died, and, as I sometimes made up my own private names for things, for some reason that I don't remember I decided to call the day on which a person died not their death day but their 'moth day' – partly I'm sure because I always found moths to be quite unpleasant – they were vague and powdery and fluttery – and they weren't horrible or terrifying, but they seemed to be blind, and I didn't like the way that they would suddenly appear and bump into me – and I guess I sort of pictured that when people died, they were sort of gently and vaguely and flutteringly escorted into death by a flock of blind moths. Well, this is all by way of saying that my own moth day, to everyone's surprise, turned out to take place only a few days before what would have been my forty-fifth birthday. I myself was certainly surprised, as the day had been, up until that particular moment, a totally ordinary day. I'd been hard at work in the morning, and then in the afternoon I'd had a rather long talk on the phone with a journalist who was writing something or other about me. And I remember that he asked me if I'd always wanted to be famous – and I'd thought, 'Always? Of course not.' Although I mean, you know, as a baby, I obviously would have come to understand, as all babies do, that if I wanted to be fed and touched and caressed, I'd better figure out how to get myself noticed, otherwise I'd starve, otherwise I'd languish all alone forever in my crib. So, that desire to be noticed obviously began fairly early, and I know that I was always an anxious little baby, and so I must also have realized pretty early that the moment I was noticed by someone, well, my feeling of anxiety, my feeling of panic, would diminish to some greater or lesser extent, and my muscles would relax, and I'd calm down. But it was only when I was sixteen years old, and I met the girl who was destined to become the center of my life, the girl I was destined to marry – Elle – it was only then that my need to be noticed became almost an obsession. Because I was desperate for Elle to notice me and pay attention to me. And I came to have a very dim, vague, not conscious awareness of the fact that if the other children in the school we attended would notice me and pay attention to me, that would inspire Elle to notice me and pay attention to me too, and that vague, dim, not conscious awareness brought about a change in my character and personality.

You see, to speak of the time before I met Elle, to speak of the year, say, when I was just fifteen years old and not yet sixteen, well, I really didn't have any friends at all in our school, and I would almost say that I didn't really have any particularly striking characteristics either. My parents were very decent, honest, hard-working people, and I suppose I aspired to be more or less like them, so I suppose there was perhaps a certain unusual earnestness in my demeanor. I didn't find it particularly funny when some of the boys stole candy from the shop around the corner from the school, and I didn't enjoy it when some of the boys started telling disgusting jokes, but I almost never talked to anyone, so no one knew I felt that way. If anyone had been forced to describe me, I guess the one thing they would have noticed about me, if they noticed anything, was that I obviously liked books, I liked to read. You know, I was a pretty sensitive, thoughtful boy who took the tests, and did well. I was the sort of boy who always kept a bunch of books in my locker, and if I had ten minutes free I'd grab a book, go into an empty classroom, and read, and that was really all there was to say about me.

The one boy I did talk to occasionally was a fairly likeable fellow in my class named Chuck. He also was rather shy and quiet, and we both sort of liked school and didn't copy other people's answers when we had to take a test, and every once in a while he and I would spend a rather aimless but rather pleasant Saturday afternoon together. You know, Chuck was rather bland, he was rather placid, but his company was very agreeable, and he was a good person to go to a movie with or take a stroll with through one of our city's parks, and for both of us our relationship was a bit like having a friend but without any feeling of being personally close. But Chuck got around a bit more than I did, and he'd gotten to know quite a number of the other students in our school, and this had important consequences for me, because occasionally he would introduce me to someone, and on one particular day he told me that he wanted to introduce me to Elle. '"L" like the letter "L"?' I asked. 'No, E.L.L.E., like "she" in French,' he said. 'Why, is she French?' I asked. 'No, but she calls herself that because she likes French things,' he said. Well, a few minutes later Chuck and I were walking down a hallway, and a bit ahead of us in the distance I saw a girl who seemed to be glittering and sparkling like jewelry, and Chuck led me up to her and introduced me to her, and that was Elle. And then Chuck seemed to somehow rather magically disappear, and Elle sort of looked me right in the face – bang, like that – and I had absolutely nothing to say – I mean, when I remember that moment, I remember myself sort of squeaking like a mouse – so she made a couple of remarks about a book I happened to be holding in my hand, and then she walked away down the hall, and I had sort of forgotten how to breathe, because during those few moments I'd fallen so very, very much in love, and I knew that something – my life, probably – had just begun, and I wasn't prepared, and I wasn't ready, and I was very frightened.

An hour earlier I'd been utterly without purpose, but now – now, the most important thing in the world was that I had to see Elle and talk to her again. And despite my shyness, I did approach her again the next day, and the day after that, and it turned out that she was the first person I'd ever met in my life who loved reading books as much as I did, and so we talked a little bit about different books, and somehow I managed to behave with a certain dignity, almost a sort of panache – I mean, I amazed myself. But Elle – my God, she was so far above me in every way. The more I saw of her, the clearer it became. She was smarter than me, and she was delicate and gentle but so much fun, so wide awake, and she was so much more active than me, more vivacious, more dynamic – she talked faster and walked faster – she was good at sports – tennis and running – and she played the oboe, she could draw, she could paint – but at the same time she was so full of emotion that she'd cry without embarrassment if she heard something sad, and above everything she was so kind, she was unfailingly kind to everyone she encountered, and she was the person people turned to if they needed advice or they just needed someone to tell their troubles to. Because she was so warm – she was warm like a furnace – and whenever I talked to her, it was as if a wave of warm air from that furnace started doing something to me, and after a while, I don't know, the blood in my veins began to circulate faster, things started moving around inside the mechanism, and slowly, gradually, the vague amoeba-like creature I'd previously been began to evolve into something with a definite form or shape. To everyone's surprise, particularly mine, I suddenly began to speak up in a few of my classes. What? Dick can talk? How is that possible? And then pretty soon I was speaking up in *all* of my classes, and then in the lunchroom, and I began to be able to talk about things, and the other kids started to be amused, sometimes, by the things I said. So bit by bit, week by week, I sort of gradually became a particular person, and that became sort of clear, first to some of the other students, and then to myself, and finally to Elle. And Elle grew to know me, and we became friends, and after a while, yes, she slowly began to care about me, and then to love me, as I'd dreamed might happen. And from that moment on, we loved each other so much, we felt that no other people had ever experienced such love before, and we studied together, we did everything together, we planned out a whole future together, and we could hardly wait for each new moment of our lives to begin.

And of course for me it was a very nice feeling to be well known in our school. And as more and more people in our school came to know me, as more and more of the students knew my name and my face, I felt less and less tense, and

I saw that there was actually no limit to just how calm and relaxed I could potentially become.

Well, anyway, on that last evening of my life I was feeling rather tired, so my plan was that I would get into bed and work for a while in bed, so I put on my pajamas, got under the covers, and picked up the manuscript of the novel I was working on, but almost immediately I fell into a deep sleep, and I began to dream, and in the dream two sentences suddenly came to me. The two sentences were, 'A couple of lambs are playing in a field. The grass is green.' And I knew exactly where I wanted to use those sentences in the novel – they were perfect – and then I started to choke, because when I tried to breathe I couldn't get any air. I couldn't get air! It was terrifying – I was suffocating. And I felt my face twisting up, sweat was bursting out of me, and my whole torso started to get hotter and hotter, and it began to hurt terribly, and then I actually felt myself dying, and then, I did die, I actually died. I died in reality. And then just a few moments later, I died in the dream. And, you know, the lights went out, to coin a phrase.

Elle Dick was a polite person, and a thoughtful person. He didn't snarl. But at totally unexpected, shocking moments I'd feel the threat of his anger, the deadly threat of it, like the feather-weight touch of a razor blade against my throat.

To be delighted by another person for a minute or two – that's something that happens. Someone caresses you. Don't ask who it is – it feels lovely. Look out your window – if you're lucky, you see a bird flying. That's wonderful – you feel it. You visit a friend, and you go into their bathroom to wash your hands, and their soap is a special color. Oh – that's nice.

Religious people speak of God's grace. For no reason you know about, God decides to give you a blessing, a gift. You can't pick the moment. God decides. To you it seems unexplainable – why now? Why me?

To be delighted by another person for a minute or two is a miracle. How is it that we were made to be able to experience that? To be delighted by another person for an hour – that's a greater miracle. Love. That comes to some people. We can't make it happen. I see you, you come into a room, I love you. That's a miracle. That's grace. I don't control that. And I keep feeling that delight, I feel it, I feel it. Today, tomorrow, the next day – then, oh, the day after that, I don't. I'm sorry, love died, it's dead. You kick it – it doesn't move. It's dead.

It's as if there was a room filled with light, and I was allowed to live in it for three minutes, three hours, three days, and then the light went out, and that room had nothing for me anymore, and I was forced to leave it.

Some people never get to go into a room like that, and some people go in for a little while, and then the lights go out, and they never experience anything like that again, and they remember that time for the rest of their lives. The time when they loved another person.

For me, starting when I first met Dick when I was just a girl, it happened quite a bit. I adored him. But then suddenly my love for him would die. It was horrible. I didn't love him anymore, and I thought maybe I never would again. But – well – I almost feel I shouldn't speak about it – but there was a trick I knew. Something I could almost do by myself, like a kind of masturbation, but I could only do it when the moment in which I could do it was somehow given to me. I'll tell you. You see, I'd be sent away from that room filled with light, sent out into pure darkness, and I'd be wandering around in the darkness, totally lost, wandering, blind, for days, until one day I'd bump into a wall with a door in it, and I'd open the door, and I'd find myself in a sort of cold, dim waiting room, and there were chairs there. And you see, I would sit in one of the chairs, and I would wait, and sometimes I'd wait for a very long time – maybe for weeks – and then I'd suddenly feel a funny sensation in my stomach, and I'd understand, Yes, now, and I had just that moment to close my eyes and do that special trick, which was partly in my mind and partly in my body, and a moment later I would stand up and leave the waiting room, and through the darkness I could see a path that went quickly back to the wonderful room in which I'd been so happy, and it was suddenly possible to go back there very easily, and the lights would be on there, and Dick would be there, and I was delighted by him again, I loved him again, and maybe I loved him even more than before. And this would happen again and again, and it was as if I got to know the way back and forth to that waiting room very, very well. And so this too was granted to me, a form of grace.

Tim Now, I know that no one's declared a holiday to celebrate the day and the moment, though maybe we should – or maybe we shouldn't – but I'm sure you occasionally think about that day and that moment, four billion years ago or so, when, out of the universe's grab-bag of ninety-nine elements, a particular selection of elements was present in the waters of the earth, and a particular sort of wind was blowing on the water, and the water had reached a particular temperature and was lit by a particular sort of ultraviolet light, and a few of those elements in the water collided with each other in just the right places so that they stuck together and formed certain particular molecules, and then after a long period of sloshing around in the water, several of those molecules bumped into each other and stuck together, and they became something that was alive. Well, I just wanted to say that those collisions that occurred in the water are sometimes called 'random' or 'arbitrary' or 'unpredictable', but they were not random, arbitrary, or unpredictable, any more than what happens when a croupier spins a roulette wheel in a casino is random, arbitrary or unpredictable. When the croupier spins the wheel and the ball lands on number twenty-four, that is not a chance event. Given the relatively fixed conditions that exist in the casino, the ball landed on the number twenty-four because of the precise amount of force the croupier applied to the spin of the wheel. The croupier couldn't tell you how much force that was, and neither could the onlookers or the players at the table, but all the same it was a specific amount of force, and given that that specific amount of force was applied, the ball could not have landed on number twenty-three. And four billion years ago, given the temperature of the water and all the other conditions, and given the particular prior events in the history of those particular elements, they had to collide, they had to touch each other in just the right places, and they had to connect and form molecules. It only took a few hundred million years, with each event in that water determined by all the events that came before it. And then a bit later the molecules had to connect and become things that were alive, and those things had to get bigger, and those bigger things had to become fish-like creatures, and the fish-like creatures had to crawl up on to the land, and some of them had to evolve to become humans, and humans had to discover fire and invent the wheel and the pretzel and the inflatable doll. Each thing that happened was inevitable, and each thing that will happen in the future is inevitable. And so my point is, the book of your life was written many billions of years ago. It was written, completed, and closed. And then locked. You're in no position to read it, but you're destined to live it. The whole story, everything that will happen to you and everything that you'll do – it's all already written in the book, down to the smallest detail. And everything that happens in the world has a chain of causes leading back from it – this was caused by this, and that was caused by something-or-other, back and back and back to the original elements and the water and the wind and the ultraviolet light.

And you see, because each of the ninety-nine elements always seems to behave in an orderly way and to follow certain immutable laws, and spherical objects always roll down hills and never roll up them, people for a long time felt that the universe was very well designed and in fact had to have been designed by a god. And actually, people used to think not only that it was designed by a god but that it was designed by a god who had benign intentions. And some people even used to say that it was designed by a god who had loving intentions. But actually it wasn't designed, it wasn't designed by a god, and it wasn't designed by a god who had benign intentions or loving intentions or any intentions. It wasn't designed at all. Each part of it follows certain rules, but the rules have no benign intention. The rules allowed humans to come into existence, to live, to survive, to evolve – they allowed all that to happen, in fact they compelled it to happen, but the rules were not benign, the elements were not benign, and there was no purpose at work there. The creature that we are wasn't made by anyone, and if you were to look at it closely as if it were something designed, as you would look at it for example if you were a teacher in a school of design, you'd have to say, 'Oh no, this is terrible, this is an appalling, dreadful design,' because the creature that we are is so full of characteristics that only a totally demented designer or a demonically evil designer would have dreamed of including in it, and one of the worst of these is the creature's ability to be hurt, to be miserable, to be in agony – an ability that, given the environment the creature lives in, is almost inevitably called into play to one degree or another by the normal daily operation and interaction of some of its other characteristics. For example, one might mention, as an inevitable source of misery for human creatures, the human's built-in need to inflict pain, to wound, to maim, to torment, to destroy, to trample, to kill, as most vividly exemplified, for instance, in the tempting activity, the tempting game, of war that the excited, drooling creature is irresistibly drawn to engage in repeatedly. Or one might alternatively look at the tempting activity, the tempting game of love or sex, to use the tiny pitiful words that the creature uses to point to invisible parts of itself, invisible parts that grow so vast that they turn us inside out and then swallow us up and eat us.

You see, each one of us is born incomplete – we wake up as someone, but we need – something – what? what is it? – something inside us tells us that, yes, we need, we need – we need *another person*, we need *someone else*, another creature, sort of like us, but not us, to lie against us, to be with us – please, please, our blood, our intestines, beg for someone, beg, scream, and then one day we find someone, we touch them, we're so happy, we're so grateful, we're complete, it's wonderful, we have everything we want . . . – but then, oh, look, wait – over there – there's something we want over there, what's happening?, we see ourselves crawling away, crawling over there, because now we feel pouring inside us some overflowing fountain of desire for something over there – what is it? – we want, we want – we want a different person, and then *another* different person, and *another* different person , and it doesn't stop, we want vaginas, penises, asses, we want to make love to dogs, to children, we want to be tied up and whipped, we want to be urinated on by him, by her – and the person we'd found at first, the one who'd made us happy, that person has to be destroyed, bludgeoned, cut into pieces. It's all built into the ninety-nine elements, all of which are bad, all of which are awful, if you think that the production of misery is awful. It's not anybody's fault. We can't get rid of the characteristics we have, we can't trade them in for better characteristics, that's just not possible. Our characteristics are mapped out in advance, the way everything is.

Dick Well, by the time Elle and I were in our last year of high school, I'd actually become a self-confident young man. I mean, she made me that, she gave me that confidence. And one day she told me, rather formally, that she thought I was a remarkable person. An unusual person. And then she said something that was almost more surprising – she said that I was a *good* person. Well, my parents really were good people, and so were hers, and Elle was obviously a good person, so I certainly liked the idea of being a good person myself. And you see, probably in Elle's mind, if I was a remarkable person, I was obviously also a good person as well, because, in her mind, those two things went together. So that was what she felt, and that's what she told me, and so why in the world wouldn't I have believed it? All right, I thought, if that's what you think, why not? Now really, I was hardly a person at all yet, I was just beginning to take the pieces of myself out of the box and put them together, so, I mean, I really didn't know what I was, and she really didn't know either, but I absorbed everything she said about me and became this rather bold character. You know, I had opinions about everything, and I loved to express them. I learned to say whatever came into my head, and I said some things that other people found interesting, and that was a great experience for me.

Well, then Elle and I got a bit older, and we went on to a big university, and we studied together there and spent all our time together, just as we had in our school. And my confidence in myself continued to grow. But after a couple of years at the university, I began to notice – well, it was almost as if in some way I was pulling some of that confidence out of Elle, the way you might pull the stuffing out of a pillow, because it began to seem as if she was becoming a bit more tentative, a bit more insecure, and a bit more dependent on me. And then in our last year of university, I started to write – very simple little stories, you know – and she was thrilled about my writing, she loved what I wrote. And then as soon as we graduated, we got married, and she got pregnant, and we had Tim. We found an adorable little apartment in the city, and we met a wonderful woman who could take care of Tim when we weren't around and would even fairly often cook our dinner. Fantastic. And then Elle decided to teach English in one of the most tormented high schools in our city, and over the next few years, because she was so much fun, and she didn't seem to get discouraged or depressed like most of the other teachers, her supervisors made sure that her classes included the most disturbed, the most unhappy, the angriest students in the school, and year after year the number of students in her classes kept on growing. And she loved her students, and she was determined to teach all of them how to write, and so every night she carried home a preposterous number of papers that the students had written, and every night she'd study them all, she'd work so carefully on every paper, and there were just too many papers, it became absurd. And every night I'd eventually fall asleep, and she'd still be working on her papers, and I wouldn't even know when she went to sleep. And of course almost all the students loved her classes and loved her, but inevitably there were some who were hostile to her – there were even a couple who threatened to punish her physically for one thing or another – and then, the building in which the school was housed was frankly terrifying. In her very first year, the boiler that heated the building exploded, and winter after winter they couldn't seem to fix it. And there were constant fights that broke out among the students – brutal fights, sometimes with weapons. And there was blood in the hallways and blood on the stairways, and people slipped on the blood and got hurt. And the food in the school cafeteria was so awful that it made the children sick. And after a few years of working at that school, Elle started to come home at night looking utterly blank, as if she'd just been punched in the face. She got thin, then even thinner, dragging herself around the apartment. And she was infuriated at herself, because she felt she was failing with this student and that student. Still, as tired as she was, she'd always spend time with Tim before he went to bed, but of course she'd usually be much too exhausted to even think of telling me what had happened during the day at school. And I'd beg her to quit her job, but she wouldn't quit.

Meanwhile I was working at a ridiculous advertising agency during the week, but every Saturday and Sunday I would go into a little room that I'd rented on the floor just below us, and I'd write. I'd just write furiously for hours at a time, because I was writing stories, and I was determined to sell them. But the thing was that on the weekends Elle wanted to be with me all the time, and that became a problem, because she didn't understand why she couldn't just sit in the room where I was writing, why she couldn't just sit there in the room and quietly read a book. Why would that disturb me? she asked. She wouldn't talk, she said, she'd just quietly read a book. Well, you know, that didn't work for me. It just didn't. I couldn't write if somebody else was in the room. And when I tried to explain that to her, she said, '"Somebody else"? What does that mean? Am I "somebody else" to you now? I thought I was a part of you, the way you're a part of me.' So, well, that was somehow the beginning of something that frankly just got worse eventually.

Meanwhile, though, I finally did start selling my stories, and she was thrilled. And then after a while I wrote my first novel, and it was actually published, and people liked it. It brought in some real money, and so I quit my job, and Elle was elated. All together, we were lucky people, and we knew that. I loved her, and she loved me. We had a wonderful son whom we both loved. And she admired my writing, and she admired me. And of course I knew it was amazing that I'd found this thing that I could do really well. I knew how rare that was. I could make up characters, imaginary beings, and put them into different situations and have them do different things that people would pay to read about. I mean, I'd actually found a professional path. And Elle was so proud of me. But there was something not quite right about it all, because it sort of came to seem as if too much of the pleasure she got out of life had to do with me and all the good things that were happening to me. On the rare occasions when we met with friends, she wouldn't talk about her work at the school – I think she felt that they wouldn't really understand what went on in that world, or maybe it was too odd for her to somehow try to pretend that her life at school had anything in common with the completely different life that our friends seemed to lead, and it reached a point that when our friends would run into her on the street, they wouldn't even ask her what she was up to, they'd only ask her what I was up to. And to be absolutely frank, I sometimes became annoyed by her, not very often, but when we were both sixteen I was never annoyed. And you might be thinking, But you were no longer sixteen, how could everything be exactly the same as it was then? But she didn't understand that – for all her brilliance she had a blind spot there, because she didn't understand why our relationship shouldn't be exactly the same as it had been back then.

Well, pretty quickly – or maybe it didn't feel quick to her – we'd both realized, after she started teaching, that the one thing she couldn't do, and wouldn't do, after a day at school, was to put on different clothes and go out with me in the evening, either to meet with friends or to go to some sort of a performance, a concert or a play or whatever. That was going to be out of the question. I mean, she was a person who had always had a lot of energy, and of course she wanted to be with me and to share with me the things that I wanted to do, but after a while I understood that it really wasn't possible, and so I stopped encouraging her or begging her to go out with me. But the truth was, now that I was spending my days all alone in a small room, well, when the evening came along I was often pretty eager to go out, so after a few years we eventually fell into a pattern in which I'd go out two or three times a week on my own, and she'd stay at home with Tim.

Elle The hours I spent when Dick would go out on the town, and I could be completely and utterly alone with Tim – those hours were sheer bliss for me. Just to be quietly alone with Tim – to look at his face, his skin. In the early days, reading out loud to him, and then later, listening to music with him, and then, still later, having long conversations with him on every sort of subject. Sheer bliss. And then of course at a certain point he'd have to go to bed. And after he went to bed I'd do my work from school, and then I'd usually get to indulge myself in my great solitary joy, because I'd get to sit on my lovely couch and read a book. And at those moments I'd feel I had the most wonderful life of anyone alive. Sometimes, though, particularly when the weather was nice, after Tim was asleep I'd leave the apartment and go out for a while and wander through the streets. And I loved to wander, and I remember feeling such enormous happiness on those beautiful nights, walking through the city. And sometimes I'd go to some sloppy place in our neighborhood and have dinner by myself.

Dick So on those evenings when I'd be on my own, I would sometimes go to listen to some music, or I'd go to a film or who knows what. But the truth was that what I really enjoyed most and what put me in the best mood was to spend time hanging out with some of the other writers or editors I'd met somehow or other during the time since I'd started writing and publishing, because it turned out that I was a rather gregarious person.

Intermission.

2

Dick Anyway, it was right around that time that Bill Bannerjee decided to come to our town for a brief visit. And you know, he always told the story of how he'd flown into town on the most beautiful spring day of the year, and he'd taken a taxi in from the airport, and he'd seen the river shining as it may never have shined on any other day before or since, and he'd seen the sunlight on the huge white buildings, and he'd seen what seemed to him to be pink flowers on all the trees, and by the time his taxi had arrived at his hotel he'd decided he would move to this country and stay here for the rest of his life. Well, I'd already read his first two novels, because even though he was very young – ten years younger than me – his work had immediately been published over here, and he'd already begun his practice of writing one short novel every single year, and, well, to me he seemed to have magical powers. His writing was just so weirdly easy to read – for our particular moment in history, his prose felt somehow uncannily comfortable. Reading it was like putting on a shirt that was an absolutely perfect fit. I mean, his writing was utterly unmannered, and yet it was somehow always unmistakably Bannerjee. Well, I couldn't explain it. Anyway, not long after he came to town he bought himself a shady little bungalow in the woods about two hours outside the center of the city, but he would always come in to the city for two or three days each week and stay in a funny small hotel he'd discovered, and eventually I met him, and pretty soon after that we had a few drinks together and began to become friends. And then not long after I first met Bill, I went out one evening to see a rather boring play that everyone seemed to love, and to my great amazement I ran into my old high school semi-friend Chuck, who turned out to be the press agent for the boring play. Well, during the intermission of the play we had an agreeable chat, and Chuck invited me to come to his apartment for a party he was throwing the following week. And so I went to that party, and, well, it turned out that Chuck had a bit of a talent for parties, and for the last few years he'd apparently been hosting these rather pleasant, rather unpretentious gatherings quite regularly in his very simply furnished, very unpretentious apartment, and there were always one or two quite interesting people there.

Tim Certainly when my father was still alive and I was a young man growing up, I knew my mother often seemed unhappy, even though I didn't know why, and I often thought about taking her away from my father. I frequently imagined going off on a very long trip on a train with her. That was a fantasy I had. And I have to say that my mother was a very attractive woman, and I did think sometimes about what it would be like to kiss her on the lips. Sure, I did think about that sometimes. And obviously I knew that I was not the only human animal on earth who was thinking about it. Mother had lovely soft lips, and the fact that every single day she carefully applied an unbelievably bright shade of red lipstick to them – well, let's be frank. Mother particularly liked men, and the daily application of that lipstick was obviously not something she did because she wanted to repel men. Because I think she particularly liked the idea that men were thinking about kissing her lips, which as I just said, was something I myself thought about every once in a while. And in addition, of course, I wondered what it would be like to touch her breasts. Yes, I did wonder about it. Though by the way, since you're so curious, I have to tell you that that was the limit of my interest, seriously. I had absolutely no interest whatsoever in having sexual intercourse with my mother, believe me, and I never thought about it for a single second. But I did sometimes think about what it would be like to go off on a trip with my mother, to sit beside Mother on a very long train ride, going off to some city neither of us had ever seen, sometimes looking out the window of the train, looking at the trees as they passed, the little towns as they passed, and sometimes not looking at anything but just enjoying the motion of the train bumping along, without even seeing anything in particular except a sort of undulating blur of color and light. And I imagined myself getting off the train with her and getting into a taxi with her and heading to some nice hotel we'd read about and selected together, and meanwhile wondering, while we were riding in the taxi, what would happen when we got to the hotel. Would we touch each other? Would we kiss?

And after the undertakers had carried Father away on the night he died, it was an amazing feeling to be sitting with her there in the dusty living room of the old apartment in a state of such tranquility. There was something absolutely fantastic about the fact that we knew that Father couldn't possibly be overhearing us as we talked. He couldn't be overhearing us, and he couldn't walk into the room and interrupt us. We could talk to each other in perfect peace. Yes, for the first time in our lives. It was incredible. Wow.

Dick When I was in my early thirties and Bill Bannerjee was in his early twenties, there was a very popular book critic, supposedly very clever, who tried to annoy me by writing an article making the case that basically Bill was a bigger and better version of me. Well, that *did* annoy me, because Bill was certainly not bigger – he was small and lightly built, but, you know, he was wiry, and not weak at all, just bantam weight. And Bill pretty much kept his private life private, but as far as I knew, he did have sex sometimes with some lucky boy or girl, older or younger. I mean, let's just say it: for a short man, he was very alluring. That crinkled, imp face was extraordinarily beautiful once you were able to read it. And when I first began to get to know him, I was entranced by the fact that he seemed to be tolerant of everyone, and he seemed to judge no one, but as I got to know him better, I realized that there were certain people he kept his distance from, and there were certain sorts of behavior that weren't attractive to him, even though it wasn't his practice to throw them down on the table and beg to discuss them. If you made an effort, you could sometimes get him to tell you about his brothers and sisters and cousins back home, and most of them seemed to be very lovely, considerate people – though not a hundred percent of them, obviously. Anyway, eventually Bill and I began to fall into a pattern of having dinner together fairly regularly on Tuesdays, and I must admit that the word 'Tuesday' did begin to have a sort of special glow for me because of that. Life could never seem dull or colorless or melancholy when Bill was around, so there was a sort of brightness that came about on Tuesdays for me. And I began to ask myself, Well, shouldn't I introduce Bill to Elle? He was so delightful, and he'd become my friend, and shouldn't I introduce him? But the thing was that Bill couldn't help being what you might call ironic – basically everything he said was ironic, which was probably why his conversation was always so delicious, and you couldn't get enough of it – but I slightly worried that what some people called Bill's 'wicked sense of humor' might rub Elle the wrong way, and I think that's why I somehow kept putting off introducing them. I mean, a lot of people who are known for their ironic manner are people who feel superior to everybody else and have a disdainful attitude about most of their fellow humans, and Elle was definitely not drawn to anyone like that. But of course Bill wasn't the least bit like that – in fact he had enormous affection for people, he didn't feel superior to anybody, and he had an incredibly kind nature – but it was true that he didn't usually show that warmer side of himself until you got to know him a bit, so I just thought, Well – I won't introduce them right away. Even though I always had a little theoretical image in my mind of how Bill and

Elle would have been laughing in corners together if Bill had been the same age as us and had gone to our school.

Anyway, the summer I turned thirty-five I'd come out with a new book, and I was feeling particularly sociable and somehow particularly restless, so I would see Bill on Tuesdays, but I also began to form the habit of dropping in on one of Chuck's parties every now and then, because Chuck was having parties almost every night now, and I began to drop in on them sometimes two or three times a week.

Elle And on those nights when Dick was out, and I'd put Tim to bed, there was a place in our neighborhood that I particularly liked to have dinner at, a funny, dark place called Manuel's where the good-looking boy in the kitchen really knew how to cook. Everything that he made was good, but his lamb stew was something I really looked forward to a lot. And one night I met someone there whom I really liked – Frank. His name was Frank. Frank. It was the summer when Dick and I both turned thirty-five, and it was a particularly beautiful summer, and I met Frank on a lovely night in early June when it was still quite chilly outside but the leaves on all the trees were bright green, and I was sitting in Manuel's enjoying my lamb stew and reading a book when all of a sudden I was startled to realize that the person at the next table was speaking to me – a man whom I'd never met, who soon explained to me that his name was Frank. Well, Frank was a tall man, a very tall man, and I could see that he had a rather expensive overcoat draped over his chair, and what he was telling me was that he'd had that lamb stew many times himself, and he thought it was great. I don't think I said anything – I just stared at him – so he went on to explain that he never missed a chance to come to Manuel's whenever he came to town, and in fact, he said, he came to town quite a lot, because he traveled all the time on business. Well, I still wasn't talking, so he went on to say that he worked for a very large company that made many different kinds of candy, including actually some brands of candy that everyone knew quite well. Oh yes, I said when he mentioned some of those brands, and as I clearly wasn't discouraging him from speaking to me, he told me a bit more about the routine of his life. I guess you'd say that he had a very languid, sort of drawling way of speaking, which was somehow very agreeable. It was clear that he enjoyed his job quite a lot, and that even though he worked quite hard in a way, it was very pleasurable for him to follow a certain fixed schedule every month and to glide along on a sort of predictable track that was comfortable for him. He'd been with this same company for many, many years, and I got the sense that his bosses must have liked him very much and paid him nicely. Well, Manuel's was a very quiet place, there was never any kind of music playing in there, and as Frank's table was quite close to mine, his voice was very quiet and pleasant, and as he spoke, his words would often sort of merge into a sort of quiet low chuckling. Well, I suppose I was pretending to be a bit uncertain or awkward about talking to this man I didn't know, but actually I felt totally at ease with him, so after pretending for a little while, I stopped doing that and just spoke to him fairly naturally. I didn't tell him too much about myself, but I did tell him that I was married and had a son, and I told him that I worked as a teacher. Well, that impressed him, and so I told him a bit about what it was like to do what I did. I told him a bit about the hopelessness of it all – the fact that the children had so little chance of having a good future, and unfortunately they knew it – and Frank seemed to understand what I was talking about, and it didn't seem to bother him that I became a bit emotional when I told him about a student of mine who'd been particularly brilliant and wonderful in my class. And I actually loved the way Frank talked about his own life, because everything in his life had apparently come about almost completely by chance, or that was how he seemed to see it, and you would almost say that he saw his whole life as a sort of rather quiet joke, a joke he found it very amusing to contemplate, even though the joke was in a way on him. He just seemed to find all the things that had happened in his life to be extremely funny – things had happened, and they seemed to be sort of arbitrary, but he'd sort of played along with them. He loved his wife, but there were three or four girls he'd liked quite a bit when he was a young man, and from the way he told the story, he might have married any one of them, and if he had, he would have loved the one he'd married just as much as he loved the woman who now was his wife. He loved his kids, but if they'd been different kids he would have loved them too. His job at the candy company was in a way utterly silly, because after all nobody really needed candy, but so long as you didn't eat too much of it, or so long as you didn't worry too much about what it might do to your weight or your teeth, a piece of candy was a relatively harmless object in the world, it was just a small nice thing you could offer to yourself when you felt you needed something privately pleasurable at some particular moment of your day. And over all the years he'd worked at this same company, he'd clearly gotten to know an amazing number of the other people who worked there, and he'd also gotten to know an amazing number of the people whom he'd met on the road, and he clearly enjoyed all these people and felt quite fond of many of them, but at the same time the way he described them was frankly hilarious. They all seemed to be incredible characters, the way he saw them. But he was also a reader, and when he was young it had crossed his mind to work for a newspaper, but somehow he'd never gotten around to looking into it, and then he'd had a friend who'd had a job at the candy company, and every once in a while he used to visit his friend at the candy company offices, and he'd had a good time there, and eventually one of the bosses whom he'd met had offered him a job there, and he'd decided to take it, and so now that was where he went on a great many of the days of his life. You know, he was a pretty smart guy, he was very well informed, he kept up with the news, and he had strong opinions, he was sort of concerned about things. Anyway, we talked for a while, and he really made me laugh the way I hadn't laughed for a long time, and I have to say, I did like him. His work was all about traveling, obviously, and I was sure he'd had some affairs along the way, maybe quite a few – you know, I thought, maybe he lived for that, it was probably important to him. But anyway I had a great time talking with him, we said good night, and I figured I'd probably never see him again, though I did remember that he was a devotee of Manuel's and went there often, so I also thought – well – who knows? So then one night about a month later, I was on my own, and I'd put Tim to bed, and I felt quite hungry, so – well – I went back to Manuel's, and there was Frank, and so he asked me, Would I possibly join him at his table? Oh no, no , I said – Oh come on, why not? Hm, good question, I thought. Why shouldn't I, really? There was no harm in it at all, so I moved to his table. And by the way, I should say that Frank was impeccably dressed, unlike some of the other people at Manuel's, and he had these wonderful, shiny, long, clean hands, with some attractive dark hairs on them – ha ha ha – so yes, I was drawn to him. I mean, I was under a lot of stress every day, and so Frank's sort of open mockery of all of life was kind of a relief, I really enjoyed it. You know, he was super perceptive, he took everything in, he noticed things about the people sitting there in Manuel's that other people wouldn't have noticed.

So after a rather long dinner we stood up from the table, and as I was about to leave he said rather boldly, 'Look, I know you'll say no if I ask you to meet me somewhere next week, but I'm just going to tell you, I'm going to be here at Manuel's at exactly this time exactly one week from now, so if your schedule happens to lead you to come here also at that particular time, then that will be a wonderful coincidence, and we might or might not decide to sit at the same table just as we have tonight.' Well, I did go back a week later, and I did sit at his table, and we shared a bottle of white wine, and I thought to myself, 'This is such a funny man, and I really like him.' Yes, he was a sweetheart, a good person. And I got a little bit drunk, and when we'd had our dinner, and Frank had told me quite a bit about his children, and I'd told him quite a bit about Tim, and we'd finished our very nice dessert, and he'd paid the bill, he asked me if I wanted to take a walk and get a little fresh air. And when he mentioned taking a walk, I knew he was staying at a rather understated but beautifully decorated hotel just a few blocks away, and I thought of how very, very nice it would be to hug him, to hold him, to lie in bed next to him, and then all of a sudden something surprising happened: the thought of sex suddenly stabbed me, right in the belly – Ouch – ouch – I wanted it. Oh God, something inside me sort of jumped up and opened its eyes – the lower half of my body, everything below my navel, sort of blinked and jolted and woke up. So Jesus, yes, it hurt to say no and to stand up sort of abruptly and awkwardly and then to sort of walk toward the door and say goodbye and give him a little wave and walk out of the restaurant. That was painful. That was very painful. Damn. And then there I was outside, and it was gently raining, and I walked home sort of – carefully. And when Dick came in, and we both got into our bed, I remember exactly what it felt like to touch him. I touched him differently from the way I usually touched him. And I felt he was flabbergasted by my touch. And I remember – yes, the look on his face when he came that night . . . And Frank never appeared at Manuel's again, not when I was there, anyway.

Dick Well, I was feeling pretty good that summer, because by then I'd sort of learned how to teach myself how to write, and I was getting better and better at it, and that was a very pleasing experience to be having every day. And at the same time people were even beginning to respect me. They started to admire me. And, you know, I never thought for one minute that the fact that I could write these books was one of the most important facts in the history of the universe. I never thought that. But I did think something like, Well, I've written these things, and people really like them, and I think I deserve a little reward for that. My mother grew up on a small farm and got up very early every morning and took care of a bunch of chickens, but I've had good luck, I've figured out how to do this thing that people enjoy, and I deserve a reward for that. And I was given a reward, I was given money. In the middle of people's lives of disappointment and unhappiness, I gave them something that they enjoyed, I gave them something that for a certain period of time actually made them happy, and they gave me money. But if the money was to mean anything, well, surely it was meant to be used by me, at least in part, to buy some things that *I* enjoyed. I mean, that was the point and the essence and the intention of the money. And after a while, after a certain amount of trial and error, I realized that one of the things that I really enjoyed was dropping in on some of the more louche, more slick, more shallow night spots and restaurants that happened to exist in the city I lived in, the city into a great many of whose windows one might peer on any given evening and very possibly find someone sitting in their favorite chair enjoying a book that somehow my luck had allowed me to write. The rather decadent venue called Arnold, for example – the restaurant-cum-night spot called Arnold, where young people did surprising things – well, Arnold was not necessarily a gathering-place that most perfectly exhibited the qualities of sweetness, gentleness, or delicacy which human beings could be said to be capable of possessing. In other words, maybe in the life of Jesus, or shall we say in some of the better moments in the life of Jesus, you could find some examples of those very special qualities. And maybe in some of the paintings of Botticelli you could find some reflections of some of those qualities. And possibly at Arnold, an expensive and sensual hangout on a sordid, violent street in a neighborhood where desperate people sold their bodies for rather large sums in order to further other people's dreams of carnal experimentation, you simply couldn't find many examples of those qualities. And possibly my books didn't offer many examples of those qualities either. But people enjoyed my books, and I enjoyed sitting around at Arnold. I enjoyed looking at the gorgeous array of human flesh, frankly, I enjoyed the décor, the lights, the colors, the shiny materials of which everything was made – the walls, the tables, even the floor. I enjoyed watching the goings-on, the things certain young people liked to do there. I even enjoyed the rich and costly food they served and the loud, throbbing music they played on their fabulous sound system. I enjoyed Arnold. Would Jesus Christ have enjoyed it? We don't know. Maybe, maybe not. Would Botticelli have enjoyed it ? We have no idea. But what I felt obliged to ask myself was, What about my wife? Would my wife enjoy it? Would Arnold be a place that Elle would enjoy? Would Elle find Arnold a congenial spot to spend an evening? You know, the chances were unbelievably slim that she would enjoy it. The odds were a million to one that she would absolutely not enjoy it. She would hate it, I thought. But at the same time I was obliged to ask myself, Would I actually even want her to enjoy it? If I brought my wife to Arnold, would I even be pleased if she took to the place? I wasn't sure. If she said she loved it, would I believe she was sincerely telling me the truth? And if I did believe her, would I perhaps think less of her? And I also wondered, If she were sitting next to me at my favorite table at Arnold, would I be able to enjoy the place myself? Would I want Elle to know how much I enjoyed it? Would I want her to see me enjoying it? Well no, not really. And yet it was so enjoyable that I wanted to share it with someone. Someone who would also enjoy it. Someone who would have no concerns at all about the fact that I enjoyed it. Someone who would have no opinions at all about what I ought to enjoy or ought not to enjoy. And one warm summer night, I dropped in on a rather lively party that Chuck was throwing, and I met Elaine. And the minute I met Elaine,

I knew that Elaine was the sort of person who would be fun to bring to Arnold. If my mother had been alive, I wouldn't have wanted to bring her to Arnold. And I didn't want to bring my wife to Arnold. But, if things were to have been a little bit different, I knew that I would have enjoyed bringing Elaine to Arnold.

Well, Elaine and I didn't get to have a very long conversation at that party, and I didn't really learn that much about her history during the course of our conversation, but the day after the party I called Chuck, and I asked him about her, and he said she was basically a recluse, and it was actually a miracle that she'd finally agreed to come to one of his parties, after more than a few invitations. Actually, from the point of view of Chuck and some of his friends, Elaine wasn't really the most agreeable person, because to them she seemed cold, and from our brief conversation at the party I could see why they felt that, but it certainly hadn't bothered me, because you probably had to be a bit cold to have the sort of dry sense of humor that she'd had, which I'd enormously enjoyed. Chuck also said that Elaine had written a murder mystery at some point in the past, and he hadn't read it, but he said he'd heard that it was quite unpleasant, and at any rate it hadn't done very well, and Elaine now made a modest living as a freelance editor. Well, as you might imagine, I did make it my business to find a copy of that murder mystery, and indeed it was extremely unpleasant – even grotesque. And I absolutely loved it.

Anyway, I went to another couple of Chuck's parties that week, and then the next week, the first one I went to, Elaine was there. Well, I thought it would give her some sort of a weird idea if I mentioned that I'd rushed out and read her book, so I didn't tell her that, but we did talk for quite a while, and she really was droll, in a way that was totally unfamiliar to me and was a surprise to me, and I just had a wonderful time talking with her. And so this became something that began to happen every week or so during that summer. And Chuck's parties were not really the greatest place to have a conversation, because they were usually pretty loud, and Elaine's voice was very quiet, almost inaudible, and she did drink quite a bit, so her speech was often a little bit slurred as well, and so it was often hard to understand what she was saying, but it seemed too much to ask her to meet me somewhere else. I couldn't really bring myself to do that, and in any case she might have said no. But – well – the other thing was that I began to realize that Elaine was – how can I say this? Well, I guess I'll just say it – Elaine was very sexy, at least to me, and after a while I began to desire her physically, if I may dare to say that. I really desired her. I wanted to see her take off those rather mannish clothes of hers, and I wanted to touch her.

Elaine I'd never been a very romantic person, and I'd always been somewhat sorry about it, but that wasn't my nature. And I'd never been the sort of person about whom people would say, 'You can always count on her in an emergency.' And frankly, I'd probably never been the best person to call if you were sick or in pain, or the best person to call if you sensed that your life was ending, and you needed someone to come over and sit by your bed, or perhaps sit right on top of your bed, or perhaps sit next to you *in* your bed, or lie next to you and hold you and comfort you as you struggled and wriggled and finally passed on. If someone you love had just died, or someone you love had just told you that they didn't care about you anymore, I would probably never have been the person you'd want to call to come over and stay up all night talking with you, or the person you'd want to have sitting in a chair near you just silently, gently sharing the room with you as you murmured quietly and cried to yourself.

Of course I've always known how to behave with respect towards another person and how to speak in a tone of voice that shows some acknowledgment of another person's pain.

But I've never enjoyed doing that. The respect I can show at a moment like that is not a true respect. Fundamentally, well, it's always basically insincere, and I've never liked being insincere, and I've never thought it was particularly nice for the other person either.

Anyway, on that first night at Chuck's I could tell that Dick found me vaguely interesting. And over the years, well, I'd read quite a number of books – I mean, that was mainly what I'd done with my life – so, when Dick mentioned a book, I knew what he was talking about, and quite often it turned out that I'd read the book, and perhaps I'd even read one or two books by the same author that Dick himself hadn't gotten around to reading yet. So, in other words, he could talk to me. And the next couple of times that we met at Chuck's I began to feel that he was amused by me, he was entertained by me. And that in itself wasn't nothing, of course, as he clearly was a person who could rather easily provide most of the entertainment he needed just by thinking his own thoughts. But certainly the first few times we talked, there wasn't any obvious feeling of sex coming from him. He wasn't a flirt. But I think there was some kind of devil in me that made him laugh, and I guess there was, somewhere in there, a little devil in him too, and the little devil in him liked the little devil in me. And you know, it's subtle, but in certain conversations, there's a sort of sex thing that you realize is there, underneath, an unconscious teasing that goes on, like in those cartoons where the little animals' tails are sliding along on the ground and then very suddenly they flick up in the air for a moment, you know, they flick up suddenly, so with certain people, well, you're sort of talking with them and chatting, and I don't know, it isn't even as dramatic as a glance or a look, I don't know what it is, but somehow it's as if they've just very briefly shifted a bit of clothing ever so slightly and exposed their genitals for a moment – and then they go right on talking as if it hadn't happened. And I began to feel that something like that was sometimes happening with him and me after we'd gotten to know each other a bit. We'd be sitting on one of Chuck's comfortable sofas, and we'd be talking about something or other we'd read, or we'd be talking about this or that person we found interesting in the news, and something like that would just quietly happen. And there began to be a sort of happy feeling in my stomach, as if something fun and nice might somehow come to pass before the summer was over.

Dick And as the weather got warmer, and the trees got to be thick with leaves, and I saw Elaine at Chuck's a third time and a fourth time and a fifth time, I began to ask myself, Well, would it really be so terrible, would it be so hideous of me, to take Elaine away with me for a weekend somewhere and go to bed with her? Would it be so unthinkable to have had sex with two people in the course of my life instead of just one? It would be so enjoyable for me, I really want to do it, and I feel I deserve to have that experience. And in what way would that hurt Elle? I asked myself. It wouldn't hurt her at all. It wouldn't have anything to do with her. How disgraceful would it really be to make up some story to tell to Elle and then just go off and spend a weekend with Elaine? That was the uncomplicated question I asked myself, because that was the state of my understanding of myself at that time in my life, and that was the state of my understanding of sex at that time in my life. And so at a certain moment one Wednesday night as Elaine and I were sitting on one of Chuck's sofas laughing about an article we'd both read that day about a writer that neither of us particularly respected or liked that much, to my total amazement I suddenly heard myself asking Elaine in a completely casual tone of voice, as if I were still talking about the article, whether she wanted to spend the next weekend with me, and in a similarly casual tone of voice, she said that she did. So that was simple. It seemed pretty simple. It seemed pretty simple to decide to do it, and then it seemed pretty simple to plan how to do it. And let's just say that neither of us was thinking on a big scale at that moment. We weren't thinking about the trajectory of our lives, our past, our present, our future. We were thinking about a weekend.

Of course it must be said that there are still some bizarre people who believe in the theory of the unconscious mind, according to which there's at least some part of us that knows exactly what we're doing when we make what we call mistakes, such as not noticing that we've dropped a lighted cigarette onto the bed before leaving the house to go down to the corner grocery store. People who subscribe to that unconscious-mind theory basically believe that the truth about the innate destructiveness of human beings is too much for us to bear, so we spend our lives covering over that basic truth with attractive lies, lies which we're constantly telling to everyone we meet, and which we ourselves are the first to believe. Well, that's a theory most people don't subscribe to anymore.

Anyway – well – whatever theory you believe or don't believe – I told Elle the next day that I would be going to some sort of literary conference out of town during the next weekend, and during the next weekend I did go out of town, but I didn't go to a literary conference, I went to a small hotel in the middle of some nice countryside with Elaine. We went away that Saturday, and we came back Monday night, and the next night was Tuesday night – and well, this wasn't part of the original plan, but, you see, this is what happened – the next night, Tuesday night, I introduced Elaine to Bill Bannerjee, and the three of us went to Arnold. And, unsurprisingly, Elaine loved Arnold, and of course she loved Bill, and so we all agreed to meet and go to Arnold again on the following Tuesday night. And that wasn't part of the original plan either, but that's how we became the Tuesday Triplets, as the staff at Arnold began to call us.

Intermission.

3

Elle You know, he was a beautiful person before that. He was a lovely, thoughtful person, so good to me, such a wonderful father. And that was really what he was like. People envied me. Every woman I knew would say to me sooner or later, 'You know, I have to admit it, I envy you.' And until then, he was marvelously honest. Totally honest. And then at a certain moment, all of a sudden, he started to say things that just didn't add up. I mean, you know, I might or might not have been as smart as he was – it's hard to say – but I wasn't an idiot. I'd always had a pretty good eye for details. And all of a sudden he was saying these things that didn't add up. Wait a minute, I'd think – I thought you said that you were with Morris last Friday afternoon, so when could you have bought that pair of shoes? Doesn't the shoe guy close at five o'clock? Well, I'd never been a suspicious person, and I couldn't believe I was suddenly thinking like that. And obviously he was not an experienced liar. I don't think he'd told a lie in his life before that. But he'd turned into a different person. He was sort of dazed, or drifting. Really, he was disoriented. He didn't know *who* he was. His whole manner was different. The way he ate his breakfast was different. He was pretending to be the same, but he wasn't the same. We'd be having a perfectly normal conversation, and his mind would just suddenly go off somewhere. Well, I tried to deny it all to myself. I considered the possibility that I was the one who was going through something. I thought maybe I'd developed some strange psychological illness, and my perceptions were distorted. But then one evening as I was coming home from work, I looked into the window of Herman's, and I saw Walter Goodman sitting at the bar having a drink with some lady, and then ten minutes later Dick came home and said he'd just been having a drink with Walter near Walter's office, and that didn't add up, and so I said, 'Dear, I just saw Walter next door at Herman's.' And I remember he said something so absurd – he said, 'What do you mean?' As I just explained, he was not an experienced liar. Ha ha ha – he didn't know what to say, so he just said, 'What do you mean?' And so I said, 'What do I mean? What do I mean? What do you think I mean? I mean, you're not telling me the truth! You're lying!' And it was as if he just fell into a hundred pieces. His voice became like the voice of a woman, screaming – I think he was crying as well, and sort of choking – and I said, 'Dear, what's wrong? What is it?' And he said, 'Darling, I'm in terrible trouble. I've fallen in love with someone. Please help me. Help me.'

Well, I would have loved to help him. I knew this wasn't something he wanted – did he want to be a married man having a sordid love affair? No – of course not. And he still loved me. He said he did, and I believed him. And I tried to be loving towards him. But you know, what could I actually do?

I mean, I did threaten him in those first few months. Oh yes, I did threaten to kill him. You know. Of course I did. And I threatened to kill her. And I remember saying to him also, 'You don't think I have what it takes to kill our child, but I do. To hurt you, I would kill our child, and I could definitely do it.' And these were all sincere threats – they weren't calculated, they came right out of my mouth with no pre-planning whatsoever. And I did keep thinking about it. All the time! I mean, once I'd started thinking about plunging a very big, very sharp knife into his chest, or waiting for *her* outside her building – and I did follow them more than once, so I knew where she lived – you know, waiting for her and going up to her and plunging a knife into *her* chest – it began to seem more and more like something I could actually do, and of course I did keep going back to the thought of, Well, it would be the end of my life, the end of the whole world in a way, but what would definitely punish him the most would be if I killed our boy, if I killed Tim. Because, you know, look at what he'd done to me. Realistically, he'd cut me open and left me to bleed to death in the street. I mean, you have to imagine what I was like when I was sixteen years old. You have to understand, I had a lot of promise. I was a very talented girl. I had a lot of talents. And by the time I was twenty, well, men – you see, men were in love with me, and they wanted me. A lot of men. All the men I knew. But he convinced me that he should be the center of my life. He convinced me. And he told me that I could have the confidence to do anything at all in my life, because the core of my life would always be unshakable, because the one thing I could always depend on, no matter what happened to the two of us – poverty, illness, persecution, oppression, war, anything – the one thing I could totally trust in this world, was his love for me. That was the one thing that would never change. That was the rock on which I could build my life.

So that night he told me about his great love for somebody else, and he couldn't explain how it could have happened. But then, well, a few months later, he quietly hinted to me that actually he'd found me somewhat possessive – there was a need to escape, in other words, a need to escape from my strangling embrace. And so I learned that I'd become a monster who strangled people. Of course, who had turned me into that monster? He had. He had taught me to be a monster, he had taught the monster to embrace, tightly, more and more tightly – he'd *trained* me. He'd trained me to worship him, to depend on him, to cling to him. And now he felt that I'd loved him too much? and I'd strangled him? How vile of him to think that, to say that. How awful that was. So at first I still sort of loved him in a way, but I couldn't really respect him anymore, you know. And I couldn't really admire him anymore. And without the respect and the admiration, the fun went out of it. The love became a horrible kind of love, it became a distasteful kind of love.

Elaine For a moment after that first weekend, Dick spoke a few times about moving in with me, and I didn't say anything one way or another, so he stopped mentioning it. I was crazy about him, and he knew I was, but sharing a bedroom with another person, much less sharing a bathroom, had never figured in any fantasy of mine, and indeed my dream since childhood had been that I could somehow earn enough money so that I'd always be able to live by myself, and I think Dick pretty quickly sensed that that was what I wanted.

The incredible fact seemed to be that Dick knew the entire truth about what I was like, and he accepted it. More than accepted it – he liked me like that. It was what he wanted – or needed, maybe. You know, maybe at a given moment a person wants a huge banquet prepared by a great chef, and maybe at another moment they just want a plain glass of water with a few ice cubes in it. Maybe someone offers them the banquet, and they just say, Thanks, that's great, but at the moment I'd be much happier if you'd just bring me a glass of water.

Elle Well, I never stabbed Dick, and I never stabbed her, and I never stabbed Tim. Instead I became a nervous wreck. I pulled myself together for a few hours each day at school, and I did my best to act normally in front of Tim, but the fact was that I was a crippled teeth-chattering nervous wreck. And the thing I couldn't bear, the unspeakable thing, was that I became so nervous that I couldn't read. I lost the ability to sit on my couch and read a book. I just couldn't do it, and that was the most terrible thing for me.

At first, Dick thought he might leave and go live with her, but he soon dropped that idea, and so he and I kept on living together. We lived together as we always had. And I couldn't imagine any other way that I could live. To use the familiar baking analogy, I was baked. I couldn't tell myself,

'Oh, the flour you used to make that dough was bad, it was poisoned flour, you should take the flour out of the cake.' Because I was already baked, and I couldn't take the flour out of the cake, it was just too late. But eventually, slowly, bit by bit, the love I'd felt for Dick began to leak out of me. It just started quietly dripping away, until it was all gone.

Dick And of course I slept at home, in our bed, next to Elle. And sometimes we made love. And of course there were nights when she would be asleep, and I would get up and go into the next room and sit on the sofa, and yes, I did cry sometimes in terrible frustration and maybe even in grief, because I needed her to love me the way she once had, and I knew she didn't, and I couldn't stand that. My life went completely gray without that. And I kept thinking that maybe if she and I could go away together somewhere on a long, long excursion, if I could convince her to go to Japan with me, or maybe to France, then maybe I could somehow win her back. Well, I knew she probably wouldn't want to do anything like that, but I kept sort of waiting for the perfect moment to ask her about it, waiting for some moment when she might possibly have said yes. And I never abandoned that idea, but the right moment never seemed to arrive. Years passed, faster and faster, and I was moving forward in my life, and that long excursion with Elle to Japan or maybe to France kept trying to catch up to me, but eventually, just before what would have been my forty-fifth birthday, that cloud of blind moths came fluttering toward me and carried me across the finish line before the excursion to Japan or the excursion to France had any chance of catching up with me.

Elle Occasionally, at first, after the night he told me about his other love, there would still be awful moments when I'd feel a sudden affection for him, like a gust of wind blowing in through some window from the past. Then I'd immediately feel sick, nauseated, and I did throw up sometimes.

I still had some kind of a life. Tim was a beautiful boy. His lips, his arms, his face – his face saved me. And some of the children at school were beautiful too. And some were so funny, they had wonderful minds. I dreamed that they would find wonderful work one day. What if their lives could be honest and tranquil? That would be great.

I could still do my job. I could still teach. But the crazy nervousness would start to pull at me almost immediately each day as I started to walk away from the school building. I'd often grab something to eat at the place on the corner across from the school. The place on the corner was a bad sandwich shop with a terrible owner who made the sandwiches himself, and they were bad sandwiches, each one prepared with a large slathering of hate, but it was very, very hard for me to eat at home. Almost impossible. So the sandwiches kept me alive.

Dick Well, a couple of years after Bill and Elaine and I started going to Arnold, the proprietors of Arnold opened up a place next door that they called very simply Mike's Next Door – I mean that was the actual name of the place. And even though Bill and Elaine and I all loved the music they played at Arnold, well, sometimes we actually would just want to have a quiet conversation together, so on those occasions we would simply go over to Mike's Next Door, because Mike's Next Door was very, very quiet. There were lovely fluffy white tablecloths on the tables there, and the floor and the walls were white as well . . . All very nice.

Now it might occur to you to ask, if you happen to remember that whole rather vague issue of human decency – 'Oh yes,' you might ask, 'by the way, where was Elle, where was your wife, when all of this was going on, when you were enjoying yourself at Arnold and Mike's Next Door?' And at the time I would have said, 'Well, as a matter of fact, Elle is sitting at home with our boy, whom she loves, and she's doing her work for school, and I can assure you that she's quite content and having just as good a time as we are.' Well, that would hardly have been a complete or honest description of things, it was sort of a lie, but that's what I would have said. Because by then I'd dropped the idea that I was a particularly good person. I didn't think that anymore. I mean, once I'd started having a love affair with Elaine, or whatever you want to call it, I knew I'd joined that rather large group of human beings who got up every day and pursued their own interests and desires, even though they knew that their particular pursuit of whatever it was – love, money, power over others, or whatever it might be – they knew that that particular pursuit might very well happen to hurt other people – hurt them or kill them or who knows what. And so yes, well, I'd simply dropped that whole idea of being a good person, I'd dropped it right down into some hole in the street, and down it had gone into the city's sewers, and no one ever saw it again. And that was sad, if you thought it was sad, or I suppose it was sad, or some people probably would say it was sad.

I mean, you know, sure, I'll admit I would have liked to be a good person. I would have liked to include that in the list of my accomplishments. And in the earlier part of my life, yes, it looked like that might have been possible. I was a candidate for that honor. I was under consideration. But then my actions removed me from the list, and eventually it became clear that that particular medal was never going to be pinned on my chest. So that was that story, the story of the medal, the story of the medal I didn't get. The story was: I didn't get the medal.

And the story of my death was even simpler. I'd always hated going to the doctor, and even though I happened to have a very nice doctor, well, now that I was more or less you might say doing whatever I felt like in my life, or that's what I felt like I was doing, I didn't go to see my nice doctor anymore. And you know, obviously over the years I'd read quite a few articles with titles like 'Is it bad for your dog to feed it candy?' And I believe the answer, a hundred percent of the time, was always, 'Yes, it's very bad to feed candy to your dog.' Well, when I was twenty I told my mother that I wanted to grow up to be a hedonist, and once I'd explained to her what that was, she didn't approve of it. But, you know, maybe it wasn't really a choice, as she thought at the time, and as I thought at the time. Maybe I was simply born that way. Maybe I was born to be a hedonist. In any case, well, you could probably say accurately enough that for a good many years I'd been living by the laws of hedonism, and well, you could probably also say accurately enough that between the heavy cream, the chocolate, the inactivity, and the alcoholism, I probably died by the laws of hedonism as well. And that was in some ways a shame – I mean people said, 'Oh, what a shame, he died young,' but on the other hand my death was not a terrible thing. My death was not awful. My death could not even be described as one of the worst moments of my life. It wasn't fun, it was actually quite painful, but it wasn't that bad.

What *was* bad, and what *was* awful, was Tim's death, and that took place just a few years after mine. I mean, Tim really did die young, and that shouldn't have happened. That was bad. But it had a horrible sort of inevitability about it, because it seemed that Tim had somehow become absolutely obsessed with this very young girl he'd met in a coffee shop somewhere, and he was taking risks that made no sense. This young girl was a student of ballet, and she had found some tiny secret room at her ballet school – maybe it was a closet of some kind, I don't know – and Tim was apparently sneaking into the ballet school every day and meeting the girl there, and I guess they would lie on the floor there and kiss and take off some pieces of clothing and touch each other – I mean, I don't know what they did. None of my business. But anyway I guess she somehow didn't bother to tell Tim that she already had a boyfriend, or that the boyfriend was quite a bit older, maybe nineteen or twenty, or that the guy happened to be actually living with her at the time in the apartment her parents were renting for her. Anyway, on a certain particular day the boyfriend was supposedly going out of town. So on that particular day Tim and the girl were kissing and touching in this tiny room or closet or whatever, and she suddenly suggested that maybe they should go over to her apartment. Well, Tim thought that was a fantastically good idea, and so off they went, but – well well – it turned out that the boyfriend had decided to change his plans, and so when the girl and Tim got to the apartment and opened the door, there was the boyfriend, sitting in the kitchen having a beer. Well, the girl tried to explain that Tim was just a friend, and so she and Tim sat down with the guy, and the three of them proceeded to have a few drinks together, but at a certain point I guess the guy began to suspect that Tim was a friend all right, but that he was the kind of friend who might well have had a certain amount of access to his girlfriend's body, and so there was some sort of confused discussion, and Tim stood up to get away from the guy, and the guy hit Tim in the mouth. Tim lost his balance, he fell, and he hit the back of his head on the sharp corner of an iron table in just exactly the wrong place, and he started pouring buckets of blood, and neither Tim nor the girl nor the guy had the faintest idea what to do, obviously, and so very quickly Tim was unconscious, and then very quickly after that, Tim was dead. So.

After his death it turned out that Tim had been writing. He'd written these odd sort of stories that you might say were supposed to be for children, except that no sane parent would allow a child to go anywhere near them. They all concerned the adventures of a sort of satyr-like figure with an abnormally long tail and – okay – an abnormally long penis. Sometimes the penis and the tail were tied together in a sort of a ring. For neatness I suppose. God help us. What do you want me to say? Anyway, if they *weren't* for children, well, I'm not sure who you would say the ideal reader of these stories might be – probably not me,

I guess, and maybe not you, I don't know – but you'd have to say, they were very carefully written. He'd worked very hard on those stories, I'm sure of that.

Tim The undertakers had probably zipped Father up in the bag and taken him away around midnight – I wasn't looking at the clock – but eventually, as Mother and I kept on talking, some very dim wisps of daylight did begin to creep through the opening in the curtains, as if the curtains were the slightly parted lips of some tired smoker who was lazily exhaling some thin wisps of smoke. And Mother had rarely asked anything of me, really, during the course of my life, but she asked me now to make some calls in the next couple of days to a couple of relatives and some of Father's friends. And then, quite soon after she made that request, she drifted into sleep right there on the couch. I covered her with a blanket, turned out the lights in the apartment, and quietly let myself out the door. Outside, I opened all my car windows and drove home in a cool breeze in a cool sort of darkness that quietly suffused with light.

Starting a bit later that morning, I did call some of the relatives to give them the sad news about Father, but the fact was that I really didn't know many of Father's friends. One whom I did know, because he'd come to dinner at our apartment once or twice when I was a bit younger, was a not particularly thrilling guy called Chuck, and Chuck was very helpful, because he knew a great many of Father's friends, and so I made a lot of phone calls in those rather unique dreamlike days, and I learned quite a few things, and one thing that certainly surprised me was that Father's best friend had apparently been the famous novelist William Bannerjee. People said that Father had really loved Bannerjee and that Bannerjee had sort of fallen apart since he'd learned of Father's death. He was inconsolable, apparently. Well, when I spoke to him on the phone, I was sort of unprepared to find that I was immediately drawn towards him in a way that rarely happens with me. Within a few minutes, I'd become sort of infatuated with him. And so a couple of hours before Mother and I were planning to go to the crematorium to send Father into the fire, I had the thought that maybe we should invite Bannerjee to come along with us, that maybe that would be important for Bannerjee, and maybe it would be something that Father would have liked us to do. I mean, it was a bit peculiar, as I'd never met the man in person, but I called Mother and asked her about it. Well, she'd never met him either, and she immediately said no, but then an hour later she called me back and said that yes, maybe it would be a good idea, as a sort of friendly gesture towards Father, and so I called Bannerjee, and he was eager to join us. And that began the friendship between Bannerjee and Mother which after a year or so became so close that more than a few people thought they were actually lovers, though I myself always doubted that. Strangely, although Mother and Father never seemed to quarrel, as far as I ever heard or observed, Mother and Bannerjee had a very tempestuous relationship over the succeeding years, including several periods when they didn't speak, but most of the time they were intimate in an almost shocking way, though they never lived together. After my own unfortunate death, they passed my very old dog Mickey back and forth between them, but, while they both liked Mickey, neither of them had any idea how to take care of a dog – that was definitely one of the many things they had in common – and Mickey passed away within a couple of years.

At any rate, not too long after we'd taken poor Father to the crematorium and burned him, I had the idea that I wanted to go see Elaine. Maybe I thought I would understand something if I did that, and maybe at that moment I felt some need to understand things. I guess my thought was that it would be a bit like visiting a crime scene where someone you love had come to a bad end – you know, the idea that facing the details of what had happened would be a help towards comprehending and accepting it. Anyway, Elaine's number was easy to find, so I called the number, and Elaine invited me to come over for a drink. It was a beautiful bright day, and Elaine's apartment was beautifully bright, and she seemed sort of amused to be in the role of a friendly, informal tour guide.

Elaine This was where he sat and drank his tea in the afternoon.

Tim (*to the audience*) I'd never seen him drink a cup of tea in my life. Tea was Mother's drink.

Elaine (*to Tim*) What's so surprising is how peaceful this place feels now that he's gone. I could never cope with his agitation. His nerves, as he would say. It was as if he was being chased by the police, and he was hiding out here. Half the time, all I could do was say, 'Wow, Dick, you'd better take one of your pills,' 'I think it's time for one of your pills, Dick.' You know, he always had that little plastic bottle in his inside pocket.

Tim He did?

Elaine Oh yes, it was like a sort of a superstitious object for him – a talisman, you know – I mean, he always kept the old bottle and refilled it with new pills. Sometimes I just couldn't help absorbing the agitation myself, so we'd both sit here buzzing. And sometimes I'd just quietly hold him in my arms, and we'd slowly breathe together, and that desperate feeling would slowly subside. You know. And now – this apartment is like a wonderful, remote little island – sun and sea breezes, even occasionally the sound of a few seagulls out the window – I love it.

Tim Hm – I always thought he was a sort of placid person. I didn't see all that.

Elaine You were lucky then. With me, he was always worried – he was someone who worried about unnecessary things. He was sort of a foolish person in some ways, to be honest. I got tired of it sometimes.

She brings over a bottle of wine and two glasses.

Is white all right?

Tim Great, thank you.

She pours wine for both of them.

Elaine Anyway, sure, he worried about everything. He worried a great deal about you, of course. He thought you were troubled or God knows what. So by the way, I know all about you!

Tim Oh?

Elaine Oh yes, I certainly do. And yet I wasn't allowed to meet you. That was out of the question. But you know? I think you and I would have liked each other. And I mean, I said to your father all the time, 'Look, I know it would be a little bit dishonest, but couldn't the three of us just secretly meet? Tim wouldn't mind. I'm sure he can keep a secret from his mother. He's probably keeping a few already. So then,' I reasoned, 'your son would get to know you a bit better, and he'd get to know me, and I'm sure he would see that I'm not a bad person, and he might even like me, and he'd certainly see that your being with me didn't reflect so badly on you either.' But – well – your mother didn't want you to know about him and me, and I guess he didn't really want you to know either. I guess he figured that if you and he and I had been secretly visiting with each other, that would add to the sneakiness and sleaziness of the whole situation, and 'sneaky and sleazy' was just not his preferred style. If it would have been possible, he would have liked his whole life to have been totally pure and clean, you know . . .

Tim Really.

Elaine Yes, really. Because he was really a very innocent person, and I think he and your mother both came from a background where they both were raised to be very decent people. And of course I didn't come from a background like that – no no. But your father was basically great about that. He knew all about what his background was and what my background was, and he didn't hold it over my head. He really didn't. But of course he knew, he knew that I was from a sort of trashy background, you know, a somewhat cheap background, what have you, and obviously he looked down on all that. I mean, he knew perfectly well that my natural style was a bit cheap, a bit trashy, because I come from cheap, trashy people. You know, I was brought up to be a little bit underhanded, I was brought up to use underhanded methods sometimes to get this or that. I mean, my father was not what you'd call a marvelous model for all of humanity, and neither was my mother, to tell the absolute truth. I would never say, Oh yes, the world would be a radiant, resplendent place if only all human beings could try to become like my marvelous father and my marvelous mother, because then humanity would walk on the path of righteousness, and God's kingdom on earth would finally be realized. I would never say that, because my father and my mother were both somewhat dishonest, they took what didn't belong to them if they had the chance, they lied quite a bit – they didn't really think, 'Oh no I won't say that, because it might not be true.' They took shortcuts, in other words. They walked across other people's property to get where they were going. And your father and your mother didn't do that. Your father and your mother would say to themselves, 'Oh no, I can't walk there, because that's not my lawn, that's Mrs Cunningham's lawn, and so I shouldn't walk on it, because there could very well be some seeds there that Mrs Cunningham planted, and if I walk across her lawn, I might inadvertently disturb some of those seeds, and so the flowers she planted there might not grow properly.' You see, that's how they both were raised – although of course the pre-eminently decent person, the most decent, the *really* decent person, was your mother, obviously. The most decent person you could ever meet on this earth, you could say, because she was a thoroughly fine and honorable person. So unlike me, you see, because I was rather trashy. I was trash, you see. That was the reality. And occasionally, just occasionally, just very rarely, just very very rarely every once in a while, I would get a whiff of that from your father, I'd just get a whiff of his quiet awareness of how he and your mother were raised and how I was raised, and I smelled it, and I very quietly thought, Well this fucking skunk looks down on me, and he thinks I'm not as good as his fucking wife, Well, think of that. So that did occasionally happen. Just occasionally it happened. Just occasionally I got the sense that maybe I just wasn't decent enough.

Tim Really, only occasionally? Because for me it was more than occasionally. That's what I was thinking every single day!: 'Wow, they're so decent, and they raised me to be so decent, and yet I'm as sleazy as they come! And they know it! And they're so ashamed of it!' And I thought that every single day!

They both laugh.

Elaine Yes, we *would* have gotten along.

Tim Although maybe it's for the best that we didn't ever meet, because the thought of it is a little bit scary. These two sleazy people. We might have become mean.

Elaine Mean! Yes! Mean! Mean!

They both laugh.

We might have somehow been mean to your mother – or even to him!

They laugh.

No, but seriously, were you ever mean to either of them?

Tim Oh no, no, I was very well behaved.

Elaine And now that he's gone, will you still be well behaved, do you think?

Tim Oh probably, yes. At least with her. I have to be. And the style, the style of behaving decently, I know that style ridiculously well, although I sort of wish I didn't. I'd sort of love to forget all about it.

Elaine No, hold on to a bit of it. I would if I were you.

Tim But of course, frankly, I mean to really lay it out there, you know, I'm seeing him now in a slightly different light . . .

Elaine You mean, because you've learned about him and me.

Tim Well, that does change how I see him, obviously. And your getting together obviously must have changed how he saw himself. And when you say that he was sometimes subtly a bit nasty to you, that was probably why.

Elaine Yes, I pulled him over to the sleazy side of the street, didn't I. Yes – a sleazy love affair. Him, of all people. But you know, I have to say – he was better than that. He knew he had no right to blame me for the fact that we got together, he struggled against the temptation to blame me for it, and he didn't blame me for it. He never did.

Tim No, he punished my mother instead. Not in an obvious way, of course. He wasn't cruel – not that I ever saw. Just cold at times. Just a little bit cold. Just suddenly, unexpectedly, a little bit cold. Ugh. What an ass he was. God, he was awful.

Elaine No, don't say that. He wasn't awful. Don't you remember him? He was a very sweet, warm, loving man.

Tim Yeah, I know. Yeah, he was. But then – why did he make everyone else so miserable? If he was so warm and loving? Do you know what I mean?

Elaine Well, I wasn't miserable. Were you miserable?

Tim Yes, I must say I was, really, although you could say, so what. I mean, so what, really. It certainly doesn't matter.

Elaine Well –

Tim But you weren't miserable. You were all right.

Elaine Well, it was the best time of my life, and I don't expect anything better will happen to me, and I'll always remember it with happiness, if we're going to be absolutely frank.

Tim Is that right.

Elaine But what made you so miserable, do you think?

Tim Oh, I don't know. I may have just envied his talent, honestly. He was an awfully good writer. And I spent an awful lot of years sort of modeling myself on him. Which is not a bad thing to do when you're a child. I mean, you know, when you're eight years old. But then at a certain point I did realize, Oh. Hmmm . . . I can model myself on him, but I can't really be *like* him, because he's a brilliant and extraordinary person, and – whoops – I'd like to be brilliant, but – whoops – I mean, I'm – whoops – I mean, I'm pretty clever, the teachers at school like me – whoops – but I'm not – quite – ergh – as brilliant as he is, and I never will be! And so that's a bad moment.

Elaine Right, but it's a waste of your time to compare yourself to some other person. I'd try to forget about him if I were you.

Tim (*to the audience*) I suppose a lot of people take alcohol for granted. I certainly don't. I know that it's a sacred beverage, and I honor it. We sat and drank for another hour, and we didn't need to talk very much. I saw why he liked her. She was a good person.

Over the next few weeks I spent quite a bit of time alone in my little house brooding about the fact that I was going to be inheriting quite a bit of money, and I thought a lot about what I would do with it. First of all, prostitutes, obviously – yum yum. Many different prostitutes, different types of prostitutes and prostitutes with whom I could do different sorts of things. Who knows? Maybe I could learn to do all sorts of wonderful things if I had some smart, committed teachers, I thought. And if I wanted friends, well, I could probably buy friends too, to be brutally honest. Because when I was in college, some of my fellow students were rather worldly and rather sophisticated, and one of the interesting things I'd learned from them was the surprising fact that very few people can resist the offer of a free dinner in a really good restaurant – even if those people already have plenty of money and don't need a free dinner. And of course I knew that the promise of a congenial crowd of interesting personalities around the restaurant table could be an enticement as well to potential friends. And if some of the interesting people around the table happened to also be somewhat attractive, possibly offering the chance of after-dinner sex to fortunate members of the party if things went the right way, then even more outstanding figures could be lured to join the group. I realized I could probably become the hub of a rather glittering social wheel, in fact, and I even began to imagine the sort of clothes I might wear on the magnificent occasions I began to imagine. I decided I'd wear much brighter colors than I'd ever worn before, which I thought could be quite a bit of fun.

And over the next few months, I did those things. I paid money for prostitutes, and I bought friends. And it worked! My life expanded. Inevitably that meant that the time I spent with my darling Rapunzel somehow had to shrink a bit, and in any case I'd have to say that she and I had probably both outgrown the old card games in a way, and yet we weren't yet quite ready to move on to the vagina and penis games that might have seemed like the logical next step. We'd still see each other on various lazy afternoons, but, you know, there was a little awkwardness about it. We'd go into her kitchen and eat some snacks, and we'd talk about this and that, but then when we said goodbye we'd hug, and that sometimes felt funny. All the same, every once in a while I did think to myself – although it turned out to be a wasted thought, unfortunately – I did think to myself that maybe in a decade or so, if I ever did that thing of moving into an apartment or a house with another person, well, maybe that other person could be Rapunzel. I'd always found it fascinating to imagine living in the same barnyard with another animal.

One night I went out to a restaurant with some of my new friends, and everyone had told me it was such a great restaurant, and we were all in a great mood. I ordered a casserole of meat with different kinds of beans and rice, and it had a very sharp sort of vile aftertaste, and I became obsessed with the idea that it was poisoning me and I was about to become seriously sick, and I didn't know what to do, and so I started to drink a whole bunch of things I wasn't used to drinking, and after a while my head was sort of throbbing, and I abruptly got up, waving very brusquely at my friends, and I left the restaurant. There was a freezing wet wind blowing through the street, and I sat down on a bench under a clump of trees, and I called Elaine. We hadn't spoken since the time several months before when I'd visited her right after Father's death.

Tim (*to Elaine*) Hey, it's me (*to the audience*) I said.

Elaine What? Tim? What is it?

Tim Yes, it's Tim. It's me. Can I come over?

Elaine What?

A pause.

Uh – sure. What's – ? – I mean, give me five minutes.

Tim (*to the audience*) I actually reached her place probably in three minutes. When I rang her doorbell, well, it was obvious she'd got up in a hurry. Her face looked smudged, and her breath smelled of sleep. She was wearing a dressing gown, probably not washed on a daily basis.

Elaine You keep awfully late hours, don't you. What's going on?

Tim I've been at a restaurant. I – I don't feel very well. (*To the audience.*) I touched her shoulder. She didn't flinch. I held her close to me. She didn't resist. I kissed her – first on the cheek, then on the mouth. I thought, Wait – what? – she was kissing me back. Then we kissed for a long time, and then we went into her bedroom, and I got into her bed, and we kissed some more. What can I say? She comforted me.

After that night, Elaine and I met each other every few months up until my death, and we had some drinks, and we really got along. And the funny thing was that we both turned out in the end to be cult writers, if you want to see it that way. We had that in common. My cult flourished briefly after I died – a nice publisher brought out my stories in a very beautiful edition with some wonderful illustrations – but Elaine was one of those people who was a cult writer, and everyone called her that, but actually she sold a remarkable number of books. Her mysteries really caught on with a lot of people. People were actually crazy about her books.

Elaine goes away.

A few months after Father's death, Mother moved into a very small, very clean, very modern apartment in an entirely different neighborhood, much closer to her school. The school building itself, by the way, was eventually condemned. The air in the building had been unhealthy for years, even decades, as the city's health officials ultimately discovered, and personally I think that that might well have contributed to the fact that Mother died in her sixties of an awful, painful, and mysterious illness. She died in her apartment, with a bunch of ex-students sitting in the room next to her bedroom. Bill had been her full-time nurse for several months, preposterous as that was in a way, because he was hardly suited for it. But to the disappointment of his readers, for the first time ever, there was suddenly a year with no novel by Bannerjee.

Anyway, Bill outlived Mother, Father, and me, and by the way, rather unsurprisingly, Elaine ultimately outlived all of us by quite a few years, because Elaine lived to be a very old woman.

While Mother was still able to do it, she would often have me over for dinner, and it soothed me so much to watch her moving around the kitchen, taking bottles and cans and jars of spices out of the cupboards. And a few times after dinner I remember that we stood together at the kitchen window, almost breathing together, looking out at the cloudy purple of the sky over the city, and the gray streets and the melancholy buildings, both of us absorbing the heaviness of it all, the weight of the buildings and the weight of all the people in their different apartments, moving around silently making their own dinners.

Tim goes away.

Elle Several hours after the undertakers had taken Dick's body away, Tim and I were still talking, and I eventually fell asleep. When I woke up, I was alone in the apartment, still sitting right there on the sofa, and sunlight was pouring into the room. I think I spent almost a whole day and part of the next night not doing anything but sitting on the couch, falling asleep repeatedly, and then waking up and thinking, 'Where am I?' And at one point on that second night I woke up, drenched in sweat, and I started walking around the dark apartment looking at things, and everything looked ruined or spoiled, as if a foul substance had been poured on all the furniture. But then I stood in a corner in the moonlight and stared at the reflections of the headlights of cars moving along the walls, and it was as if I'd prayed to God for a miracle, and God had answered my prayer. It seemed almost impossible – I was finally free from the old life. Yes, it was completely over. Not sort of over. Not half over. Completely over. Dick was gone, and I'd never have to see him or think about him ever again. And all the questions – when he comes in the door, how should I greet him? should I hug him? should I kiss him? what should I say to him? – all the questions had been wiped away. It was as if I'd been in one of those terrible dreams in which there are agonizing, impossibly complicated problems that you have to solve, and then you wake up, and you can hardly believe it, but hooray! it was a dream, and you don't need to solve those problems at all! And for so many years, in order to bear it and keep going, I'd had to whisper to myself constantly all day long, 'I don't really live in this apartment, I'm just pretending. I'm not really connected to this man, I'm just pretending.' And now I didn't need to pretend anything to anybody, and I didn't need to say anything to anybody that I didn't want to say.

Finally, I opened the bedroom door and went into the bedroom. Then I went into the bathroom, and I brushed my teeth, and then I dressed for bed, and I got under the covers of the bed, and for a moment I felt the twinge of a funny sensation in my stomach, and I remembered that there was once a time when I could will myself into a special state, a state of love, but I didn't want that now, and I could feel the sensation in my stomach quietly fading away as a wonderful calmness and blankness fell over me. And then a great excitement began to fill my whole body as I began to think about the life I might now be able to live. I thought about a sweater I wanted to wear. A sweater, a skirt. And I thought about the music I wanted to listen to. And – and the books I wanted to read . . .

Elle goes away.

Dick While Elle was still alive, and particularly during the period when Elle was sick, Bill didn't see Elaine all that often. He still would visit her occasionally in her sunny apartment, and they still enjoyed each other's company very much, but the crazy excitement that Bill and Elaine and I had felt together wasn't there, obviously, and after I died neither Bill nor Elaine ever went back to Arnold. Arnold was my place. Once a year or so, Elaine would go to one of

Chuck's parties, and on one occasion she persuaded Bill to come along with her, but Bill was bored at the party, and he couldn't really deal with it, so he left pretty early, and he never went back to another party at Chuck's.

End.